Weiss Ratings' Consumer Guide to Variable Annuities

Weiss Ratings' Consumer Guide to Variable Annuities

Spring 2018

GREY HOUSE PUBLISHING

Weiss Ratings
4400 Northcorp Parkway
Palm Beach Gardens, FL 33410
561-627-3300

Independent. Unbiased. Accurate. Trusted.

Published by Grey House Publishing, Inc., located at 4919 Route 22, Amenia, NY 12501; telephone 518-789-8700. Grey House Publishing neither guarantees the accuracy of the data contained herein nor assumes any responsibility for errors, omissions or discrepancies. Grey House Publishing accepts no payment for listing; inclusion in the publication of any organization, agency, institution, publication, service or individual does not imply endorsement of the publisher.

4919 Route 22
PO Box 56
Amenia, NY 12501-0056

Spring 2018 Edition

ISBN: 978-1-68217-816-4
ISSN: 2164-8255

CONTENTS

Terms and Conditions

Weiss Ratings' Mission Statement

Weiss Ratings' mission is to empower consumers, professionals, and institutions with high quality advisory information for selecting or monitoring a financial services company or financial investment. In doing so, Weiss Ratings will adhere to the highest ethical standards by maintaining our independent, unbiased outlook and approach to advising our customers.

Weiss Ratings'
Consumer Guide to
Variable Annuities

In the rush to build up enough assets for retirement, consumers are faced with a dizzying array of investment choices. What's more, the "correct choices" for someone else may be totally inappropriate for you. Consider the following factors that could impact your own investment decisions:

- How much risk you're willing to take
- Your age and the number of years you have until retirement
- Your income level and tax rate
- The financial needs of others who may depend on you
- Other investment alternatives available to you now
- Your accumulated assets and personal net worth
- How much income you feel you'll need or want to receive during your retirement years

And when you consider the vast number of investment vehicles, each designed to address one or more of the above factors, the task of making a decision can become mind-boggling. At Weiss Ratings, we believe that the best decisions are informed decisions. Therefore, this guide is designed to help you fully understand the pluses and minuses of at least one of those investment vehicles: **variable annuities**. That way, you can decide for yourself whether or not an investment through variable annuities is right for you.

Before Even Considering Variable Annuities ...

Most people recognize that, when planning for retirement, tax-deferment is a powerful investment strategy. The compounded growth of your investment is magnified when taxes are not deducted annually. And you are likely to be in a lower tax bracket during your retirement years, thus preserving still more of your nest egg. The hard part is figuring out which tax-deferred vehicle is best for you. What you may not know is that there are two tax-deferred investment vehicles that are almost always preferable to all of the rest.

Company-Sponsored Retirement Plans

Pre-tax investments in company-sponsored retirement plans (such as a 401k, 403b or 457) are one of the *best* ways to lower your present income taxes and accumulate retirement money. These plans often have company matching contributions up to a certain level, offering you free money in addition to the advantages of tax deferral. Furthermore, most companies nowadays give you investment choices, which by the way, are usually fairly similar to those available in a variable annuity.

The only major drawback is that the government limits the amount of pre-tax dollars you can contribute. In addition, some individual plans may be unattractive if they are charging you too much in cost or imposing restrictions on your ability to get to your funds without first leaving the company. Generally speaking though, company-sponsored retirement plans present a superior investment opportunity. Therefore, in nearly all cases, before investing for retirement using a variable annuity, you should first contribute as much as you possibly can to any company-sponsored retirement plans available to you.

IRAs

After maximizing your contributions in work-sponsored retirement plans, the next best alternative is an Individual Retirement Account (IRA) - preferably at a discount broker that offers low yearly fees and low trade commissions. The costs associated with maintaining an IRA are very low (often free of annual fees for balances over $10,000) and many discount brokers offer a wide array of no-transfer-fee, no-load mutual funds and low commission levels when investing in stocks.

Unfortunately, your annual tax-deductible contribution to a regular IRA (as well as your total annual contribution to a Roth IRA) is limited and becomes phased out at upper income levels. Nevertheless, use them as much as you can because they offer a great deal of investment flexibility at little or no cost.

Now, <u>after</u> investing to the limit in company-sponsored retirement plans and your IRA, you are ready to consider variable annuities.

Who Should Consider Variable Annuities?

Investing in variable annuities is very similar to investing in a company-sponsored retirement plan or IRA. Variable annuities allow you to manage your funds as you choose by selecting the mutual fund investments that suit your personal risk tolerance and wealth-building needs. But there are a few significant differences you should be aware of:

Difference #1. A major advantage: There are no limits on the amount of money you can contribute to a variable annuity.

Difference #2. A major disadvantage: All money you contribute to a variable annuity is *after taxes.*

Difference #3. Insurance: Variable annuities have an insurance component not found in other types of retirement investments. This can make the annuity more attractive if you need and want the insurance, but less attractive if you don't. (More details on this aspect later.)

Before Retirement

A variable annuity may be a prudent investment once you have already contributed the maximum amounts allowed to your company-sponsored retirement plan and IRA. Even though your contributions to a variable annuity are after taxes, the annuity's earnings will be allowed to grow tax free until you begin to make withdrawals. At this stage, it's called a "deferred annuity" because any payments back to you are deferred until some point in the future. And should you die before retirement, the entire investment will be passed on to your designated beneficiary or your estate.

After Retirement

A variable annuity can also be an appropriate investment vehicle if you have reached retirement age and need to roll your savings out of a 401k or other company-sponsored retirement plan. You can move the funds into a variable annuity where they will retain their tax-deferred status while allowing you to begin using your retirement savings for your living expenses. This is called an "immediate annuity." You pay in a lump sum, and you begin receiving a monthly stipend immediately.

Your immediate annuity can either be fixed or variable. The fixed variety guarantees you a fixed monthly payout amount for the remainder of your life. In contrast, in a variable annuity, your monthly stipend will be periodically adjusted based on the performance of your investments. Many investors opt for the variable annuity, even though the payout is not guaranteed, because stock market equity investments have historically outperformed all other investments.

There's no guarantee this will continue to be true in the future, however. Indeed, a long bear market could actually lower the income you receive from an immediate variable annuity. Thus, variable annuities offer the prospect of higher payouts in the underlying investments, provided they're timed properly, while the guaranteed payouts in a fixed annuity stay at the same level for as long as you live.

What Are Variable Annuities?

Variable annuities were first introduced by insurance companies back in 1954. The idea was to create an alternative to the industry's existing product offerings which, at the time, were all based on fixed contributions resulting in fixed payouts. The fixed annuities were very popular. But the insurance companies couldn't help noticing the rising popularity of mutual funds. They wanted to compete with mutual funds by offering policyholders the potential for higher earnings. Variable annuities provided the answer. They maintained most of the attractive features of the traditional fixed annuity. Plus they allowed investors to choose from a range of mutual funds.

How Variable Annuities Work

When You Buy a Deferred Variable Annuity

First, the insurance company invests your money into the mutual fund or funds you designate, recording a corresponding liability to you, the policyholder. Unlike money you invest in a fixed annuity or a whole life insurance policy, variable annuities are managed by an investment company using mutual fund "subaccounts" that are kept <u>totally separate</u> from the insurer's other assets. Therefore, your funds are not subject to claims by its creditors should the company become insolvent. In that sense, a variable annuity is much safer than a fixed annuity or even a life insurance policy. The risk you take is primarily due to any risk in the mutual fund investments you choose.

From that point forward, all income you earn is tax-deferred. You pay no income taxes on it until you begin making withdrawals at retirement. Furthermore, if you are unfortunate enough to suffer an early demise before retirement, the insurance company will pay your designated beneficiary or estate the net balance of your accumulated contributions (less withdrawals) plus any earnings. Unlike a term life or whole life insurance policy where you pay in a small amount to guarantee a large death benefit, the insurance aspect of variable annuities merely guarantees payout of the money that has been invested plus the accumulated gains.

There's one more built-in cushion: Let's say you invest most of your money in stock market funds and the market takes a tumble. Plus, let's say you pass on before retirement and before the market recovers. Your designated beneficiary or estate is guaranteed to receive *at least the net amount you paid into the annuity - with no deductions for the decline in the value of your investments*.

"Annuitizing" to Create an Immediate Annuity

So far, we have equated your date of retirement with the date you start collecting your annuity - called "annuitizing." But it doesn't have to be at retirement. You can decide to annuitize whenever you want. Once you make that decision, the insurance company guarantees to send you periodic payments for the remainder of your life and, in some cases, beyond depending on the payout option you choose. Generally speaking, the payout options available to you are:

- "Individual" - pays until your death
- "Joint and survivor" - pays until the death of both you and your spouse
- "Joint life" - pays until the death of you or your spouse, whichever comes first

In addition, each of these options also has sub-options which further define how long the benefits are paid. These include:

- "Pure life" - pays for the remainder of your life, however long or short that may be, but terminates with no residual value upon your death
- "Period certain" - pays for the remainder of your life or a pre-determined number of years, whichever is longer
- "Refund" - pays for the remainder of your life, and guarantees the return of your net contributions to your heirs if you die prematurely

We can't tell you which payout option is best for you. It's a complex decision based on your individual income needs and how important you feel it is to pass along an inheritance to your heirs. Consequently, we recommend you consult with an independent financial planner for a more complete explanation of the options available to you in order to determine the payout that will best suit your needs.

One word of warning: Once you annuitize an annuity, the investment is moved from the separate subaccount to the insurance company's own pool of assets. So at that point, it does become critical that you monitor the financial stability of your insurer. If the company fails, it will certainly curtail your ability to get to your funds on a timely basis and may even impact the amount of money you receive.

Illustration: The Power of Tax Deferment

Let's say you want to make a one-time investment of $20,000 and then see what happens under two scenarios - one utilizing the tax-deferred power of a variable annuity, and another using an ordinary taxable mutual fund where the owner receives and reinvests an annual distribution of earnings. For the purposes of this illustration, we're going to assume you have a marginal tax rate of 24% and you earn an average annual net return of 4% on each investment. However, dividend distributions from the taxable mutual fund (excluding a money market mutual fund) are subject to a maximum 15% tax rate for taxpayers earning up to $428,800 ($479,000 for married persons filing jointly) per year effective January 1, 2018 in accordance with the American Taxpayer Relief Act of 2017. Also, in order to simplify the illustration, we'll assume there are no sales commissions, loads, or other annual fees for either type of investment vehicle.

	Investing in a Variable Annuity	Investing in a Taxable Mutual Fund
Initial After-Tax Contribution	$20,000	$20,000
x Annual Return	x 4%	x 4%
First Year Earnings	$800	$800
x Marginal Tax Rate	N/A	x 15%
Taxes Owed after First Year	$0	$120
Investment Value after One Year	$20,800	$20,680
Investment Value after Ten Years	$29,605	$27,941
Investment Value after Thirty Years	$64,868	$54,531

As you can see, the effect of compounding returns on the tax-deferred variable annuity really magnifies your investment growth. Now let's look at what happens when you decide to draw down your accumulated investment from 30 years of saving over a fixed 15-year period during retirement.

	Investing in a Variable Annuity	Investing in a Taxable Mutual Fund
Investment Value after Thirty Years	$64,868	$54,531
Annual Payout over 15 Years	$5,834	$4,905
Taxable Portion of Annual Payout	$4,037	avg $1,269
x Marginal Tax Rate	x 24%	x 15%
Taxes Owed on Annual Payout	$969	avg $190
Annual Payout after Taxes	$4,865	$4,715

Based on this example, you would receive $150 more per year during retirement over the 15-year payout period by investing through a variable annuity.

One more big difference: With the annuity, the longer you live the more total benefits you get. Without the annuity, you run the risk of running out of money just because you've been fortunate enough to enjoy a long life.

An Alternative to Annuitizing

Here's a commonly employed strategy which allows you to periodically receive a portion of your funds, while retaining your rights to the remainder of your net contributions and earnings. This strategy involves annually withdrawing only a portion of your funds after you have reached age 59 ½, and not annuitizing the annuity. Most insurance companies permit you to withdraw up to 10% of the value of your annuity annually without incurring a penalty. And once you reach age 59 ½, there is no danger of an early withdrawal penalty from the IRS.

Therefore, this strategy allows you to withdraw the same amount the insurance company would have paid you each year had you annuitized the annuity. However, the assets in the annuity remain yours to be passed on to your heirs and are not at risk in the event of the insurance company's bankruptcy.

The drawback to this strategy comes if you outlive your life expectancy and your withdrawals deplete the assets in your annuity. So if you're healthy and anticipate this possibility, you would probably be better off annuitizing promptly and letting the insurance company accept the responsibility for making the payouts.

More Advantages of Variable Annuities

We've told you about the two main advantages: 1) the tax-deferred growth for building up your retirement nest egg, without sharing a portion of your earnings with Uncle Sam each year along the way, and 2) the ability to sock away as much as you want and use it to cover your retirement or pass it along to your heirs.

Plus, consider these additional benefits that come with a variable annuity:

Guaranteed Return of Funds at Death

The insurance associated with deferred variable annuities provides that if you pass away before annuitizing, the insurance company will guarantee payment of the total value of your variable annuity or entire amount of your premiums paid in, if greater, to your designated beneficiary or estate. Furthermore, if your designated beneficiary is your spouse, many variable annuity contracts have a feature which allows the spouse to either maintain the variable annuity as is, or to roll it over into another variable annuity under his or her own name.

The Potential for Investment Diversification

Most variable annuities offer a variety of mutual funds to meet your individual investment goals and comfort-level with risk. Indeed, the best variable annuities will offer at least seven mutual funds to choose from, including:

- an aggressive growth fund
- a growth fund or S&P 500 index fund
- a growth and income fund or balanced fund
- a small cap fund
- an international or global fund
- a bond fund
- a money market fund

Many also offer an emerging market fund, a high-yield bond fund and a value fund. The more fund choices, the greater flexibility in shaping your investment strategy and coordinating variable annuity investments with your investment in taxable accounts and company-sponsored plans.

Asset Protection: Your Savings Are More Secure from Lawsuits

If someone sues you, it is much more difficult for them to recover money you keep in an annuity, either fixed or variable, because it is technically part of your <u>insurance</u> contract.

If you like this feature and it's important to you, it would be a good idea to consult with an attorney; your success in shielding a variable annuity investment from a lawsuit will depend largely on your individual circumstances. But there can be no doubt that an annuity offers greater potential for asset protection than other investments.

Guaranteed Lifetime Withdrawal Benefits

Guaranteed withdrawal benefits can come in a variety of ways, but the most common is the guaranteed lifetime withdrawal benefit which guarantees that a certain percentage can be withdrawn each year until you die. The amount that can be withdrawn is determined at the time you begin making withdrawals based on your age and the amount of the guaranteed withdrawal benefit value that has accumulated in your contract since its inception.

The guaranteed withdrawal benefit value is the value that your account has grown by a guaranteed percentage rate each year regardless of the movements in the market. This is different than your account value which fluctuates with the performance of the underlying investments and is the amount that you would receive if you surrendered the policy. The beauty of the guaranteed lifetime withdrawal benefit is that it does not go down if the performance of the underlying investments goes down.

Protection from Insurance Company Failure

Your subaccounts in a deferred variable annuity are invested through a trustee, which legally protects you from a failure. Just a year or two ago, this may not have seemed to be a great advantage, because large company failures were rare. But in today's uncertain environment, this can be very important. And in the early 1990s, many large annuity companies went under, trapping more than one million fixed annuity investors in a moratorium, with many forced to accept losses of up to 50 cents on the dollar. In contrast, variable annuity investors were safe and had immediate access to their money even if their company was in bankruptcy.

Disadvantages of Variable Annuities

Market Risk

The biggest potential disadvantage to variable annuities is the possibility of a decline in the market value of your investments. While the insurance company will guarantee the return of 100% of your net contributions should you die prior to annuitizing, an overall long-term decline in the financial markets would effectively eliminate the principal advantage of tax-deferred growth. If there is no growth in the value of your investment, it really does not matter whether or not it is tax-deferred. A long-term down or flat market would also mean you incurred opportunity costs compared to the guaranteed growth available with a fixed annuity or other type of fixed-income investment.

In addition, should you decide to annuitize your investment and maintain it as an *immediate variable annuity*, a decline in the value of the underlying investments would result in a decline in the amount of your periodic payouts. So, with an immediate variable annuity, you get the prospect of increasing the payments you receive based on the market's performance, but you also accept the risk of decreasing the payments as well.

Requires Hands-on Investing

With a variable annuity, you can't just make your investment and forget about it. You need to monitor the financial markets and modify your mutual fund investment choices as conditions change. This requires certain financial skills plus a minimum amount of time and effort. If you are already investing through taxable mutual funds or directly in the stock market, there is no additional effort required. However, if you are not a hands-on investor and you neglect your variable annuity, you risk serious disappointment.

You Are Paying for Insurance Too

To guarantee the return of your principal, the insurance company is naturally going to charge you a premium. This insurance cost, in turn, dampens the overall return of the variable annuity. So if you feel you already have sufficient assets or life insurance to cover the needs of your loved ones, the additional insurance provided by a variable annuity may not be worth the dampened returns you will experience.

Tax Considerations

Income Taxes on Withdrawals and Payouts

Regardless of your age at the time of the withdrawal or payout, you will be required to pay regular income taxes (at your then-current tax rate) on the accumulated earnings portion of the amount you receive.

Any withdrawals made prior to annuitizing the contract will be considered first to come from earnings, not principal. However, periodic distributions, that is distributions that are annuitized, are taxed differently as shown below.

Furthermore, if you *withdraw* money prior to age 59 ½, the IRS is generally entitled to 10% of the earnings portion of the withdrawal as a *penalty*. So, if you are in the 24% marginal tax bracket, the government is going to take a total of 34% of the accumulated earnings portion of the withdrawal amount. In addition, state income tax and penalty will be owed depending on your state of residency. That can be a high price to pay in order to gain early access to your own savings.

Separating Return of Principal from Accumulated Earnings

Since you have already paid taxes on the principal that you originally contributed to the annuity, the government will not penalize you or tax you on that portion of your withdrawals or payouts. But you must not forget to deduct the amount of your principal when preparing your income taxes.

How do you know what portion of a withdrawal or payout is accumulated earnings and what portion is after-tax principal? The IRS uses the following formula:

Nontaxable return of principal =
$$\text{annual payment} \times (\text{principal paid in} \div \text{total expected return})$$

In this formula, the *principal paid in* equals the total amount you have contributed through a lump sum or periodic contributions.

For a deferred annuity, the *total expected return* is the current value of the entire annuity. When performing this calculation on an immediate annuity, the *total expected return* equals the annual payment guaranteed by the insurance company times your number of years of life expectancy remaining. Since life expectancies vary by individual, the IRS maintains a set of annuity tables for determining your life expectancy based on your current age.

Example: Determining the Taxable Portion of a Payout

Let's walk through an example to clarify the calculation. Jane Smith is a 69-year-old woman who has contributed $100,000 to her annuity and is just starting to receive monthly payments.

The IRS annuity tables show that she has a life expectancy of 17 years; and the insurance company calculates that she should receive $12,000 per year in monthly payments of $1,000 each. So her ...

Annual payment = $12,000

Principal paid in = $100,000

Total expected return = $204,000 ($12,000 annual payment x 17 year life expectancy)

As a result, the ...

Nontaxable return of principal = $12,000 x ($100,000 ÷ $204,000) = $5,882.35

Thus ...

Taxable return of earnings = $12,000 - $5,882.35 = $6,117.65

In this example, Ms. Smith only owes income taxes on $6,117.65 of the $12,000 annual payment she receives from her annuity. The $5,882.35 is considered a return of her original after-tax contributions. And if Ms. Smith is fortunate enough to live a long and happy retirement past the age of 86, the insurance aspect of the policy guarantees that she will continue receiving her monthly payments for the rest of her life. From a tax standpoint, however, all of her original principal is returned to her over the course of her remaining 17 years of life expectancy. So any payments she receives after age 86 will be considered completely taxable income.

Estate Taxes

If you pass on before annuitizing your annuity, the entire value of the annuity is included as a part of your taxable estate - unless you have designated your spouse as the beneficiary. If you die <u>after</u> annuitizing, the estate tax implications vary depending on the payout option you've selected.

The simplest case is when you select a "pure life" payout. The annuity contract is essentially terminated and any remaining assets in the policy are forfeited to the insurance company. The estate gets nothing and pays nothing.

In contrast, if you're single and select a "period certain" payout, any unpaid funds remaining are included as a part of your estate and paid directly to your beneficiary. For example, if you select a "15-year certain" payout option and then pass away after only 12 years, the payout for the remaining 3 years is included in the estate's value, but payable directly to the beneficiary.

Variable Annuity Mutual Fund Subaccounts

Mutual Fund Offerings

In the past, most insurance companies had in-house investment companies to manage their mutual fund subaccounts. To remain competitive, however, most now offer a wide variety of funds managed by big, well-known mutual fund companies - Janus, Templeton, T. Rowe Price, Vanguard, Fidelity, and others. They do this by simply creating "clones" of their regular mutual funds and then dedicating the clones strictly for the variable annuities. These funds use almost the same portfolio allocations and are generally run by the same managers as the regular mutual funds.

Even though the funds are clones, the performance is not identical however. Returns can be higher - or lower - depending on how closely the mutual fund manager is able to mimic the regular mutual fund's investments. Generally, the difference over time is negligible.

Evaluating Mutual Fund Performance

We recommend you evaluate the mutual funds in two areas: (1) rate of return compared to funds with a similar investment make-up, and (2) costs imposed by the fund.

Morningstar contains one-year, three-year, five-year, and 10-year performance figures as well as benchmarks based on the average performance for all similar-type funds. These benchmarks are especially helpful for evaluating a particular fund relative to its peers. Morningstar also publishes its own rating system evaluating the mutual fund subaccounts and ranks similar-type funds by performance over various time horizons.

The average annual returns for variable annuity mutual funds for 2016 and the previous five and ten years is shown below. (Note: Extremely poor stock market performance in late 2008 and early 2009 has skewed the 10-year results lower):

Fund Type	1-Year Average Annual Return 2016	5-Year Average Annual Return 2012-2016	10-Year Average Annual Return 2007-2016
Aggressive Growth Funds	7.02%	10.02%	4.67%
Growth Funds	7.58%	10.86%	5.09%
Balanced Funds	8.83%	8.66%	3.86%
Small Cap Funds	17.3%	12.24%	5.97%
International Funds	1.69%	5.00%	0.79%
Bond Funds	4.90%	2.06%	3.31%
Money Market Funds	-1.24%	-1.28%	-0.56%

Never forget, however, the all-important warning that <u>past performance is no assurance of future results</u>. After an unusually long bull market and a decade of low interest rates, the results of 2008 demonstrate that it is more important than ever that you not rely too heavily on the past.

Costs Compared to Taxable Mutual Funds

The costs associated with variable annuities can be a definite drawback. Indeed, high-cost variable annuities take 12 to 13 years before they catch up to the after-tax returns you can get from an equivalent taxable fund. In other words, if your intention is to invest for short periods of time, you'd be better off investing directly in mutual funds and paying the taxes.

Fortunately, some variable annuities let you in with no up-front load and let you out with no surrender charge. Furthermore, they cut the break-even point when compared to taxable mutual funds down to a two- to six-year time horizon. These low-cost variable annuities are sold directly by mutual fund companies or by the insurance company themselves, so there's no need to go through an insurance agent, unless you're uncomfortable handling the paperwork by yourself.

Switching Between Funds

To make the most out of your annuity, you need the flexibility to switch among the seven investment options mentioned in the *Evaluating Mutual Fund Performance* section above - from an aggressive growth fund to a safe money market fund.

Remember, the more fund choices, the greater the flexibility in targeting your investment strategy and coordinating with your investments in taxable accounts and company-sponsored retirement plans.

Favor a variable annuity that allows you to transfer from one fund to another with the lowest cost and greatest speed - to respond readily to changing market conditions and changes in your personal situation. You should be able to call up the insurance company and give instructions to sell one fund and buy another, and get same day executions, just as you would with a regular mutual fund.

Variable Annuity Costs

As you can see, the best variable annuities will have low costs while giving you a wide variety of mutual funds to choose from. Getting a handle on the true costs though, is tricky. Generally speaking, variable annuity costs show up in four forms:

- the mutual fund's annual expenses (mostly going to the mutual fund manager)
- insurance expenses to cover the death benefit premiums and administration costs
- commission loads covering the sales cost
- an annual contract fee

Mutual Fund Annual Expenses

At first glance, a mutual fund annual expense may appear to be higher than that of a variable annuity and that's because many mutual funds already include a portion or all of the insurance expense. Variable annuities can have annual and insurance expenses shown separately calling for a careful review when determining the final cost. So, if you want to know the true amount of a mutual fund annual expense, simply check the one with the lowest annual expense ratio; on the other hand, in order to arrive at the final cost of a variable annuity, you must add all expense items together to see the total annual expense ratio.

Fund Type	Variable Annuities	Taxable Mutual Funds
Fund annual expense	1.00%	2.00%
Insurance	1.18%	0.00%
Total	2.18%	2.00%
Difference	0.18%	

According to industry-wide figures, the average annual expense ratio for variable annuity fund subaccounts is 1%, compared to 2% on taxable mutual funds. But, after adding in all the other costs for insurance including administration and distribution, the average expense for variable annuities jumps to 2.18%. This is why the final cost of an investment must be examined very carefully to avoid any hidden or unexpected fees.

Front-End Loads

The front-end load is the commission you pay out of your investment contribution. It goes to cover sales costs, especially the fee paid to the salesperson who sells you the policy. For example, when you buy a variable annuity with a 4% front-end load, $4 of every $100 you put into the policy goes to the sales costs, with only $96 actually credited to your account.

That's why we recommend only no-load annuities where there is no up-front reduction in your principal. You do pay a slightly higher cost built into the mutual fund expense or insurance expense, which comes out of your earnings over time. But since every penny that you invest gets credited to your account, all your funds start working for you immediately. Good news: Over 97% of the variable annuities sold today have no front-end loads.

Surrender Charges

Another major charge that you should look out for is at the back-end surrender charges. Although they can take many forms, most surrender charges are designed to discourage you from making withdrawals during the first few years after you purchase an annuity. The typical charge starts at 7% in the first year, declining 1% annually over the course of the first seven years of the policy. This means that if you make a withdrawal or cancel the policy in the first year, the insurance company will keep 7% of your total investment. In the second year, the charge drops to 6%, and so on until it reaches 0% after seven years. Some annuity issuers have altered their surrender charges so that they <u>do not</u> decline to 0%, but only decline to 1-3%, a setback for unaware consumers. Moreover, for many policies <u>each time you contribute new money into your policy, this "seven-year clock" starts afresh for the newly invested portion</u>.

Some variable annuities also carry "rolling surrender charges," meaning that even your investment gains, as they accrue to your account, are subject to the terms of the surrender charge! Under these contracts, a certain amount of the value of your policy will <u>always</u> be subject to a surrender charge no matter what. The only way to get out of this trap is to annuitize the policy.

Ideally, the best kind of variable annuity to own is one without any surrender charges. This may be somewhat difficult to find on your own. But in a moment, we'll give you the names of some no-load, no-surrender-charge policies on the market today.

Annual Contract Fee

Most variable annuities assess an annual contract fee of $25 to $35. This flat rate fee guarantees the issuing insurance company that it will receive an annual stream of revenue regardless of the size or performance of your personal variable annuity. Unfortunately, there is very little you can do to avoid this charge. Still, it's not a factor you can ignore when comparing variable annuities with one another and with other types of investments.

Bottom Line

It definitely pays to shop around and compare variable annuities based on their costs and performance. But when comparing costs, remember that you must factor in the insurance costs and loads associated with the annuity to get the full picture.

Don't Ignore the Stability of the Insurer

Even though you may buy an annuity through your broker, bank or mutual fund company, variable annuities are issued solely by insurance companies. This means that the safety of the insurer cannot be ignored.

Also, keep in mind that a financially troubled insurance company may be looking for ways to cut corners. Oftentimes, this could mean a decline in the quality of service it provides you. While this risk is not necessarily financial in nature, it is real - and it can result in some frustrating experiences for you.

Regardless of whether you are considering a variable or other type of annuity, the best and safest practice is to stick with annuities issued by financially sound insurers. That way you will not have to worry about the safety of your investment or the consequences of the company's failure. After all, there are plenty of good, financially strong insurance companies issuing attractive annuities. So, why take a chance with a weak insurer? It just doesn't make sense.

Weiss Ratings offers a number of services designed to inform investors and professionals alike about the financial condition of an insurer.

For more information on these and other products offered by Weiss Ratings, call 1-877-934-7778 or visit www.weissratings.com.

Selecting a Variable Annuity

Are Variable Annuities Right For You?

Now that you are familiar with how variable annuities work, including their inherent advantages, disadvantages, tax considerations, and mutual fund considerations, you are in a much better position to determine whether or not they're right for you. Keep in mind though, it is usually a good idea to consult a professional such as a Certified Financial Planner before making any major moves in retirement planning.

You Should Consider Variable Annuities If:

1. You can make a long-term financial commitment for retirement, and you are confident that you won't need access to your money before you retire.
2. You have already fully funded any company-sponsored retirement plans or IRAs for which you are eligible.
3. You can take full advantage of tax-deferred growth of your investments. This is especially appropriate if you are in - or entering - a high marginal tax bracket and are at least six years away from retirement.
4. You need to shelter your savings from potential lawsuits and make it less accessible to the courts.
5. You feel up to making your own investment decisions, or alternatively, you have a financial advisor you can rely on.
6. You have already established a source of liquid assets that you could tap in case of an emergency. Remember, it will be costly if you ever need to withdraw money from an annuity before retirement.

You Will Probably Want To Avoid Variable Annuities If:

1. You have not yet fully funded any company-sponsored retirement plans or IRAs available to you.
2. The ups-and-downs of the stock market make you nervous and you are averse to the risks associated with mutual fund investing.
3. You know little or nothing about mutual fund investing and are not interested in learning.
4. There is a good chance you will need the money before retirement for living expenses, emergencies, long-term care or other investment opportunities you may want to pursue.

Ten Steps in Evaluating a Variable Annuity Policy

Once you decide that investing in variable annuities is the correct choice for you, you should follow these steps before buying:

1. Shop around. There are so many variable annuity products on the market today that it pays to take the time you need to find the one that best suits your needs.
2. Avoid all variable annuities that charge a front-end load. The up-front cost just cannot be justified.
3. Favor annuities with no or low back-end loads (surrender charges) unless guaranteed withdrawal benefits are one of your requirements. Most, although not all, variable annuities with guaranteed withdrawal benefits charge a surrender fee for a certain number of years.
4. Focus first on those insurance companies with a Weiss Safety Rating of A (excellent) or B (good). Since the variable annuity will be maintained as a "separate account," you may also decide to consider companies with a C (fair) rating, although you will want to periodically monitor them more closely.
5. Avoid variable annuities that do not offer a choice of at least seven mutual fund subaccounts - an aggressive growth fund; a growth fund or S&P 500 index fund; a growth and income fund or balanced fund; a small cap fund; an international or global fund; a bond fund; and a money market fund.
6. Compare the performance of the funds available through the variable annuity to the averages for those types of funds. You should look for variable annuities with funds that have achieved at least average performance for the last one-year, three-year, and five-year time horizons. It is a good idea to look at long-term results to get a sense of how well the subaccounts have performed over time.
7. Compare the variable annuities' total expense costs. (Total expense = mutual fund annual expense + insurance expense). Look for variable annuities that have total expenses at or below the industry average of 2.18%.
8. Make sure the variable annuity allows you to switch between the mutual fund subaccounts by telephone, preferably at no additional cost.
9. Favor a variable annuity policy that gives you the right to withdraw up to 10% of your money annually with no surrender charge or other penalty. You may never take advantage of this feature, but it is good to have in case of emergency.
10. Look for variable annuities offering a periodic step-up of the insurance amount as the value of the mutual fund subaccount grows through the years.

Excellent Variable Annuities on the Market Today

Here we present two lists of best annuities recognizing that investors may have different priorities. The first list of variable annuities meets virtually all of the criteria on the previous page with a heavy focus on keeping expenses down. They have no front-end load, below-average costs, a wide selection of mutual fund subaccounts with good performance, and are issued by insurance companies rated A (excellent) or B (good) by Weiss Ratings.

When considering these annuities, be sure to make comparisons based on the funds' total cost (insurance cost + annual expense), the availability via an IRA account or group retirement plan, and any other features that might meet your specific needs.

The Best Low-Cost Variable Annuities					
Name of Variable Annuity Name of Insurer Phone Number	Front-End Load	Surrender Charge/ Years Applies	Number of Funds	Number of Strong Funds	Weiss Safety Rating
• **Ameritas Advisor NO-LOAD (6150)** Ameritas Life Insurance Corp (402) 467-1122	None	None	65	45	B
• **ForeRetirement IV VA I** Forethought Life Insurance Co (812) 933-6600	None	None	51	31	B
• **Northwestern Mutual Select-Fee Based 2006** Northwestern Mutual Life Insurance Co (414) 271-1444	None	None	41	31	A-
• **Schwab Advisor Choice** Great-West Life & Annuity Ins Co (303) 737-3000	None	None	108	81	B-
• **Smart Track** Great-West Life & Annuity Ins Co (303) 737-3000	None	None	110	81	B-
• **Smart Track Advisor** Great-West Life & Annuity Ins Co (303) 737-3000	None	None	97	77	B-
• **Symetra True VA** Symetra Life Insurance Co (425) 376-8000	None	None	119	92	B+
• **Thrift Plan/457 FDA/Trad, Roth,Inherited IRA** Mutual of America Life Insurance (212) 224-1879	None	None	40	31	A-
• **TIAA Access 1** TIAA-CREF Life Insurance Company (212) 916-4900	None	None	64	39	B
• **TIAA Access 2** TIAA-CREF Life Insurance Company (212) 916-4900	None	None	48	26	B

The second list of variable annuities contains those with some type of guaranteed withdrawal benefit. We feel it is important to find good annuities with this feature because contract holders receiving guaranteed withdrawal benefits were insulated from the drastic decline in the stock market during 2008 and early 2009. Some investors may find such a benefit a worthwhile trade off for the additional fees it may add. These additional fees include surrender charges and internal fees specific to the guarantee; however, the annuities in this list have total expenses at or below the industry average for all annuities.

Again, when considering these annuities, be sure to make comparisons based on the funds' total cost (insurance cost + annual expense), the availability via an IRA account or group retirement plan, the type of withdrawal benefit that suits your goals, and any other features that might meet your specific needs.

The Best Variable Annuities With Guaranteed Withdrawal Benefits					
Name of Variable Annuity Name of Insurer Phone Number	Front-End Load	Surrender Charge/ Years Applies	Number of Funds	Number of Strong Funds	Weiss Safety Rating
• **Advisor's Edge** Transamerica Premier Life Insurance Co (319) 355-8511	None	None	50	31	C+
• **Fidelity Freedom Lifetime Income** Fidelity Investments Life Ins (617) 563-9106	None	None	9	6	A-
• **Monument Advisor** Jefferson National Life Insurance Co (502) 587-7626	None	None	411	265	C
• **Vanguard Variable Annuity** Transamerica Premier Life Insurance Co (319) 355-8511	None	None	17	16	C+

Note: In arriving at the above list of "best" variable annuities, mutual fund subaccount performance played an important role in the selection process. After all, a variable annuity can have low costs and a strong Safety Rating, while at the same time offering only mediocre fund performance. Likewise, when researching other variable annuities, you will want to include in your evaluation the performance of the funds in which you are interested. Policies are listed in alphabetical order.

Data source: Weiss Ratings and Morningstar.

The Worst Variable Annuities on the Market Today

The following variable annuities possessed one or more drawbacks which made them unattractive investment options at the time of this publication.

The Worst Variable Annuities						
Name of Variable Annuity Name of Insurer	Front-End Load	Surrender Charge/ Years Applies	Number of Funds	Number of Strong Funds	Weiss Safety Rating	Primary Draw-backs
• **MetLife Growth & Income NY-J** Metropolitan Life Insurance	None	2% 5 years	2	None	B-	Limited and weak fund choice, Surrender charges, underperforming
• **MetLife Growth & Income NY-S** Metropolitan Life Insurance	None	2% 5 years	2	None	B-	Limited and weak fund choice, Surrender charges, underperforming
• **Prudential Defined Income** Pruco Life Insurance	None	7% 7 years rolling	2	1	C+	Limited and weak fund choice, Surrender charges, underperforming

Note: The above list is intended to provide a sample of those variable annuities that contain one or more unattractive features. Exclusion from this list does not mean that a particular variable annuity is a good investment choice. Likewise, some of the insurance companies listed above offer several additional variable annuity policies which may be worthy of consideration. Policies are listed in alphabetical order.

Data Source: Weiss Ratings and Morningstar.

What Our Ratings Mean

A   **Excellent.** The company offers excellent financial security. It has maintained a conservative stance in its investment strategies, business operations and underwriting commitments. While the financial position of any company is subject to change, we believe that this company has the resources necessary to deal with severe economic conditions.

B   **Good.** The company offers good financial security and has the resources to deal with a variety of adverse economic conditions. It comfortably exceeds the minimum levels for all of our rating criteria, and is likely to remain healthy for the near future. However, in the event of a severe recession or major financial crisis, we feel that this assessment should be reviewed to make sure that the firm is still maintaining adequate financial strength.

C   **Fair.** The company offers fair financial security and is currently stable. But during an economic downturn or other financial pressures, we feel it may encounter difficulties in maintaining its financial stability.

D   **Weak.** The company currently demonstrates what, in our opinion, we consider to be significant weaknesses which could negatively impact policyholders. In an unfavorable economic environment, these weaknesses could be magnified.

E   **Very Weak.** The company currently demonstrates what we consider to be significant weaknesses and has also failed some of the basic tests that we use to identify fiscal stability. Therefore, even in a favorable economic environment, it is our opinion that policyholders could incur significant risks.

F   **Failed.** The company is deemed failed if it is either 1) under supervision of an insurance regulatory authority; 2) in the process of rehabilitation; 3) in the process of liquidation; or 4) voluntarily dissolved after disciplinary or other regulatory action by an insurance regulatory authority.

+   The **plus sign** is an indication that the company is in the upper third of the letter grade.

-   The **minus sign** is an indication that the company is in the lower third of the letter grade.

U   **Unrated.** The company is unrated for one or more of the following reasons: (1) total assets are less than $1 million; (2) premium income for the current year was less than $100,000; or (3) the company functions almost exclusively as a holding company rather than as an underwriter; or, (4) in our opinion, we do not have enough information to reliably issue a rating.

Once You Choose a Variable Annuity

Manage Your Money Wisely

Do your homework when evaluating your mutual fund choices and diversify your asset allocations among several funds with the best track record. You certainly do not want to purchase a variable annuity with the anticipation of significant investment growth and then select mutual funds that cannot deliver. And yet, many people buy a variable annuity policy and then leave their assets entirely invested in money market funds. Get the most out of your investment by being proactive in evaluating your investment choices.

Most investment advisors recommend coordinating variable annuity investments with all other investments you hold. Younger investors are usually advised to stake more in the stock market while retired investors should usually follow a more conservative asset allocation. You may want to consult a professional, such as a Certified Financial Planner, to help determine the asset allocation that is right for you.

Stay abreast of the financial stability of your insurance company. We recommend that you maintain your variable annuity and other policies with A (excellent) and B (good) rated companies whenever possible. You can monitor the safety of your insurer by looking up ratings for free at www.weissratings.com. Also, many public libraries carry Weiss Ratings' *Guide to Life and Annuity Insurers*, a quarterly publication containing ratings for almost every insurance company in the nation.

In the event that your company's rating drops to a C (fair), do not rush out immediately and transfer your investment to another insurer. Instead, look at the whole picture, including the returns and costs associated with the annuity issued by the insurer, before considering a change. If the company moves into one of the "weak" categories (Weiss Safety Rating of D or E), however, you should seriously consider making a change.

Exchanging an Existing Variable Annuity for a Better One

If you happen to stumble upon a variable annuity that is more attractive than the one you already own, or if your current variable annuity's returns and/or costs take a turn for the worse, you may want to consider moving your investment. Here's how:

First, make sure the switch is worth it given whatever surrender charges you will incur. If the back-end load is significant but on a declining scale, you may want to delay the change to avoid or reduce the surrender charge.

Second, contact the insurance company you want to switch to and ask them to provide you with the necessary forms for a *1035 tax-free exchange*.

Then, simply fill out the necessary forms and return them to the insurer issuing the new variable annuity policy. They will take care of the rest, including the actual transfer of your money to the new policy.

Other Annuities and Similar Products

Variable annuities are certainly not the only vehicles available to you for use in your retirement planning. So do not allow yourself to be swayed by a salesperson's pitch directing you to one type of investment over another. Instead, decide for yourself what product best suits your needs and then use the salesperson as a resource to help you find the best deal for you. Here are some of the alternative, and yet similar, investment choices along with the relative advantages and disadvantages of each compared to variable annuities. You may want to consult your accountant or Certified Financial Planner if you have questions beyond the scope of what's addressed here.

401(k) Plans

If your company offers a 401(k) plan and you are eligible to participate, it is certainly worth investigating. A 401(k) plan allows you to make an elective pre-tax contribution of up to 100% of your annual salary ($18,500 for 2018 and if age 50 or older, you can add $6,000 for a total of $24,500) into an investment account for retirement. In addition, many employers offer matching contributions up to a certain level as an inducement to participate in the plan. This amounts to free money just for participating, and is over and above the elective employee limits.

Your contributions (and your employer's matching contributions) will grow tax free. When you withdraw them, however, you will have to pay taxes on the entire amount of the withdrawal. And if you make a withdrawal prior to reaching age 59 ½, you may also have to pay a 10% penalty to the IRS. Plus, most employers impose an additional restriction on the portion they contribute to your 401(k) by subjecting you to a vesting period; if you leave the company before a certain number of years, a portion of these matching contributions will be withheld.

Like variable annuities, most plans offer an array of mutual funds to choose from and allow you to switch monies from one fund to another at no cost. Since your employer selects the manager for the 401(k) plan, however, you have no say over the quality of the funds available to you in terms of their performance and costs.

Advantages vs. Variable Annuities

Advantage #1. Your contributions to a 401(k) plan are before taxes (whereas contributions to a variable annuity are after taxes). Thus, <u>the 401(k) plan gives you a tax break in the current year</u> - a feature which is not available through a variable annuity.

Advantage #2. Company-matching contributions. Not all 401(k) plans offer this, but you should certainly take advantage of this attractive feature if it is available to you.

Advantage #3. Most 401(k) plans offer a loan feature, giving you quick access to cash with no pre-qualifying conditions and no IRS penalties. Variable annuities do not offer this type of temporary access to your money.

Disadvantages vs. Variable Annuities

Disadvantage #1. The government limits the amount of pre-tax dollars you can contribute to these plans. Therefore, if your retirement goals require investing more than the yearly maximum ($18,500 for 2018; plus the applicable catch-up contribution for anyone age 50 or older), you may need to supplement these with other investments.

Disadvantage #2. Some individual plans may be unattractive compared to variable annuities if they incur extraordinarily high costs or they impose severe restrictions on your ability to get to your funds without first leaving the company. Every plan is different. So you will need to weigh your own employer's plan against your other investment options.

Disadvantage #3. Your investment choices are limited to the funds your employer has selected.

Example

Let's assume John Smith is employed by ABC Manufacturing Company, where he is paid an annual salary of $50,000. And let's compare two scenarios: one where he annually contributes 15% of his pre-tax salary to a company-sponsored 401(k) plan; and the other where he takes the same amount, pays taxes on it, and then invests it through a variable annuity. For the purposes of this example, assume that the net rate of return for each of these two investment vehicles is the same at a conservative 4%, and Mr. Smith is in the 22% marginal tax bracket.

	Investing in a 401(k) Plan	Investing in a Variable Annuity
Annual Salary	$50,000	$50,000
x Contribution Percentage	x 15%	x 15%
Annual Contribution Amount	$7,500	$7,500
x Marginal Tax Rate	N/A	x 22%
Taxes Owed	$0	$1,650
Annual Contribution Amount after Taxes	$7,500	$5,850
x Annual Return	x 4%	x 4%
Investment Value after One Year	$7,800	$6,084
Investment Value after Ten Years	$93,648	$73,045
Investment Value after Thirty Years	$437,463	$341,221

As you can see, your investment will grow much faster when you can fund it with pre-tax dollars through a company-sponsored 401(k) plan. And if your employer offers matching contributions, the results are magnified even further. Now, let's assume Mr. Smith has reached retirement and decides to convert his investment from 30 years of savings into an immediate annuity with a fixed 15-year payout.

	401(k) Plan Investment	Variable Annuity Investment
Investment Value after Thirty Years	$437,463	$341,221
Annual Payout over 15 Years	$39,346	$30,690
Taxable Portion of Annual Payout	$39,346	$14,905
x Marginal Tax Rate	x 22%	x 22%
Taxes Owed on Annual Payout	$8,656	$3,279
Annual Payout after Taxes	$30,690	$27,411

Based on this conservative example, Mr. Smith would receive $3,279 more per year during retirement by investing through a 401(k) plan than he would by investing through a variable annuity. And if you assume a more aggressive 7% annual return, this differential widens to $10,043 per year. These results are magnified even further for individuals in higher tax brackets.

Who Should Consider 401(k) Plans?

Everyone who has this investment option available to them should seriously consider saving for retirement through a 401(k) or similar company-sponsored retirement plan. If your company does not offer one, speak with your Human Resources Manager and suggest they start a plan immediately. It's a shame not to take advantage of the tax savings the IRS has made available to you and your company.

Regular IRAs

Individual Retirement Accounts are available through a number of sources including most banks and brokerage firms. Those IRAs offered by discount brokers provide you with the most investment flexibility and are generally free of any annual fees if your IRA balance is more than $10,000. Furthermore, many discount brokers offer a wide array of no-transfer-fee, no-load mutual funds and low commission levels when investing directly in stocks.

The IRS limits your annual IRA contribution to a maximum of $5,500 per person for 2018 (age 50 and older can add $1,000 to the limit for a total of $6,500). If you are not participating in a retirement plan at work, the entire amount of this contribution is tax-deductible, meaning you do not owe taxes on that money in the current tax year. However, if you are in a work-sponsored retirement plan, then the tax-deductibility of your contribution begins to phase out for 2018 when your modified adjusted gross income (MAGI) exceeds $63,000 per year ($101,000 per year for a couple). If only one spouse is covered by a retirement plan at work, you can deduct up to $5,500 ($6,500 for 2018 if age 50 or older) in an IRA for the uncovered spouse, if MAGI is under $189,000 (phased out completely at $199,000).

As in other retirement vehicles, your contributions will grow tax free until you withdraw them, at which time you will be required to pay taxes on the entire amount of the withdrawal (excluding any amounts for which you have already paid taxes). And if you make a withdrawal prior to reaching age 59 ½, you may also owe a 10% penalty to the IRS.

You can make penalty-free withdrawals from your IRA to pay for your education costs or the education of your children or grandchildren. You may also withdraw up to $10,000 from an IRA to purchase a first home for yourself, your children or your grandchildren without incurring any penalties. You will still owe taxes on these early withdrawals, but the IRS will waive the 10% penalty.

Generally, the IRS requires that you begin making at least minimum withdrawals from your IRA by the time you reach age 70 ½.

Advantages vs. Variable Annuities

Advantage #1. Regular IRA contributions are before taxes. As you will see in the next example, the benefits of this can be substantial.

Advantage #2. There are no insurance expenses weighing down the performance of your investment with an IRA.

Disadvantage vs. Variable Annuities

The government limits the amount of pre-tax dollars you can contribute for 2018 to an IRA to $5,500 per person ($6,500 if age 50 or older) or $11,000 per couple ($13,000 if both age 50 or older) per year or less depending on your income level. You may need to supplement these savings with other investments in order to have sufficient income during retirement.

Example

Let's assume that over a 30-year period of time, Patty Jones saves $5,000 per year toward her retirement under two scenarios: one where she makes pre-tax contributions to a regular IRA; and the other where she takes the same amount, pays taxes on it, and then invests it through a variable annuity. For the purposes of this example, assume that the net rate of return for each of these two investment vehicles is the same at a conservative 4%, and Ms. Jones is in the 22% marginal tax bracket.

	Investing in a Regular IRA	Investing in a Variable Annuity
Annual Contribution	$5,000	$5,000
x Marginal Tax Rate	N/A	x 22%
Taxes Owed	$0	$1,100
Annual Contribution Amount after Taxes	$5,000	$3,900
x Annual Return	x 4%	x 4%
Investment Value after One Year	$5,200	$4,056
Investment Value after Ten Years	$62,432	$48,697
Investment Value after Thirty Years	$291,642	$227,481

As you can see, your investment will grow much faster when you can fund it with pre-tax dollars through a regular IRA. Now, let's assume Ms. Jones has reached retirement and decides to convert her investment from 30 years of savings into an immediate annuity with a fixed 15-year payout.

	IRA Investment	Variable Annuity Investment
Investment Value after Thirty Years	$291,642	$227,481
Annual Payout over 15 Years	$26,231	$20,460
Taxable Portion of Annual Payout	$26,231	$9,937
x Marginal Tax Rate	x 22%	x 22%
Taxes Owed on Annual Payout	$5,770	$2,186
Annual Payout after Taxes	$20,461	$18,274

Based on this example, Ms. Jones would receive $2,187 more per year during retirement by investing through a regular IRA than she would by investing through a variable annuity. This result is magnified even further for individuals in higher tax brackets.

<u>*Who Should Consider Regular IRAs?*</u>

As with a 401(k), everyone whose annual income level permits them to take full advantage of a pre-tax IRA contribution should consider doing so.

Roth IRAs

The Roth IRA was first enacted in 1997, and modified with expanded limits through passage of the Taxpayer Relief Act of 2001. At first glance, the Roth IRA appears to be similar to a regular IRA.

- You are limited to an annual contribution for 2018 of $5,500 per individual ($6,500 if age 50 or older), which is phased out at upper income levels (see below). Similar to a regular IRA, the annual contribution is limited to taxable earned income.
- The method of investing and investment options through a bank or discount broker are the same.
- You owe no taxes on your annual earnings in either IRA.

In reality, however, the Roth IRA has several key features which make it much more attractive than a regular IRA, or a variable annuity for that matter.

First and foremost, you fund a Roth IRA with after-tax dollars, and in turn, owe no taxes on your withdrawals. Thus, you forfeit any tax advantages in the current year, but more than make up for it by avoiding taxes on your principal and earnings when you withdraw them.

Second, after five years, the IRS permits you to withdraw any amounts that you have contributed to a Roth IRA - tax-free and penalty free - *under certain circumstances.* For instance, a young couple could contribute to a Roth IRA over several years and then withdraw the entire amount of their contributions to fund the purchase of a house, while leaving their accumulated earnings in the account to continue growing tax free.

Third, the modified adjusted gross income (MAGI) levels used for determining your ability to make a Roth IRA contribution are different from MAGI levels used for Regular IRA contributions. Individuals making less than $120,000 can contribute up to a full $5,500 for 2018

($6,500 if age 50 or older), which is phased out completely at $135,000 annual income. The same goes for couples making less than a combined $189,000 (phased out completely at $199,000). For a married individual filing a separate return who is an active participant in an employer-sponsored retirement plan, the phase-out range is from $0 to $10,000 annual income.

One other consideration: Unlike a regular IRA, the Roth IRA does not require you to make minimum withdrawals when you reach age 70 ½. There are no required withdrawals associated with this investment, and you can pass it on to your heirs completely income tax free (the amount will still be added to your taxable estate for estate tax purposes).

Advantages vs. Variable Annuities

The prospect of tax-free withdrawals and payouts represents a significant advantage for Roth IRAs over variable annuities. Both investments are funded with after-tax dollars so there is no advantage there, but the tax-free payouts in later years can make a big difference in the amount of money you will actually receive.

Disadvantage vs. Variable Annuities

The only drawback to a Roth IRA is that the government limits the amount of your 2018 contribution to $5,500 ($6,500 if age 50 or older) per person, and $11,000 per couple ($13,000 if both age 50 or older) per year or less depending on your income level. Therefore, you may need to supplement these savings with other investments in order to have a sufficient income during retirement.

Example

Let's assume that over a 30-year period of time, Tom Johnson saves $5,000 per year toward his retirement under two scenarios: one where he makes after-tax contributions to a Roth IRA; and the other where he contributes the same amount through a variable annuity. We'll also assume that the net rate of return for each of the two investment vehicles is 4% and Mr. Johnson is in the 22% marginal tax bracket.

	Investing in a Roth IRA	Investing in a Variable Annuity
Annual Contribution	$5,000	$5,000
x Marginal Tax Rate	x 22%	x 22%
Taxes Owed	$1,100	$1,100
Annual Contribution Amount after Taxes	$3,900	$3,900
x Annual Return	x 4%	x 4%
Investment Value after One Year	$4,056	$4,056
Investment Value after Ten Years	$48,697	$48,697
Investment Value after Thirty Years	$227,481	$227,481

As you can see, the value of your investment remains the same regardless of whether you use a Roth IRA or a variable annuity because they are both funded with after-tax dollars and you pay no taxes on either's annual earnings. Now, let's assume Mr. Johnson has reached retirement and decides to receive his investment from 30 years of savings over a fixed 15-year payout period.

	Roth IRA Investment	Variable Annuity Investment
Investment Value after Thirty Years	$227,481	$227,481
Annual Payout over 15 Years	$20,460	$20,460
Taxable Portion of Annual Payout	$0	$9,937
x Marginal Tax Rate	N/A	x 22%
Taxes Owed on Annual Payout	$0	$2,186
Annual Payout after Taxes	$20,460	$18,274

Based on this example, Mr. Johnson would receive $2,186 more per year during retirement by investing through a Roth IRA than he would by investing through a variable annuity. This result is magnified even further for individuals in higher tax brackets during retirement.

Who Should Consider Roth IRAs?

Clearly everyone whose annual income level permits it should consider contributing to a Roth IRA. Even though you will likely want to supplement your IRA savings with some other form of retirement savings, you should still take advantage of this opportunity.

Indexed Annuities

At first glance, indexed annuities (also called equity indexed annuities) appear to provide investors with the best of all worlds. These investments are set to appreciate at the same rate as a stock index, usually the S&P 500 index, over the term of your policy so you can enjoy the upside potential of investing in stocks. And should the stock market turn bearish during your policy term, they eliminate the downside potential of a loss by guaranteeing a minimum annual return, usually 3%.

Sound too good to be true? Well, in most instances, it is. Here's why:

First, your returns on an indexed annuity will never equal the returns you would get from owning an S&P 500 index mutual fund. Reason: Although the annuity provides you with the S&P 500's price appreciation (historically averaging about 7.5% per year), it does not include the index's dividend returns (which have averaged about 3%). So whereas an investment in an S&P 500 index fund has historically provided investors with an average total return of about 10.5% annually, an indexed annuity would only have given you about 7.5%.

The frequency with which your interest is credited is another potential pitfall. Indexed annuities that only credit your earnings at the end of the policy term are at a serious disadvantage. Even if the stock market has a couple of great years in the early part of your policy term, those returns could be completely wiped out in the latter years of this type of policy, leaving you to rely on the 3% guaranteed minimum return for nominal investment appreciation. In other words, most policies do not give you a minimum return based on the greater of 3% or the performance of the S&P 500 each year. Instead, you receive a return based on the greater of 3% compounded annually or the long-term performance of the S&P 500. This leaves you very vulnerable to an untimely cyclical stock market downturn.

Another downfall is that the guaranteed minimum return is not paid on your full investment. Regulators require that the guaranteed minimum rate be paid on either 87.5% or 90% (depending on the state the annuity is sold in) of the original principal. Therefore, in reality you are getting even less than the stated minimum guaranteed return. On an initial investment of $100,000, a 3%

guaranteed minimum return would be paid on either $87,500 or $90,000, which would be $2,625 or $2,700, respectively, rather than the $3,000 you might expect.

Finally, your investment safety with an indexed annuity is far more dependent on the financial stability of the underwriting insurance company. Unlike a variable annuity, your funds are pooled with the assets of the insurer. If the insurance company should fail during the term of your policy, your funds could be subject to a moratorium on withdrawals.

You would think that your investment is going into an S&P 500 index fund. In reality, the insurer typically invests about 70% of your money in bonds and 20% in call options on the S&P 500 index, with the balance going toward acquisition costs, administrative costs, and insurance company profits. If interest rates drop and the stock market stagnates or declines, the insurance company will be saddled with a loss. Unless it has a good capital cushion or good revenues from other sources, it could be hard-pressed to pay you what it promised.

If you already own an indexed annuity, be sure to consult the issuing company's Safety Rating so you will know the risks you are taking with this type of investment.

Advantages vs. Variable Annuities

The most obvious advantage is the guaranteed minimum annual return. This safety net is one that many people find attractive. In recent years, companies have started offering guaranteed minimum accumulation benefit riders on their variable annuity policies, which guarantees that the contract value will be at least equal to a certain minimum percentage (usually 100%) of the amount invested after a specified number of years regardless of the underlying investment performance.

Disadvantages vs. Variable Annuities

Disadvantage #1. Your returns will always be lower than a comparable investment through a variable annuity because you miss out on the dividends.

Disadvantage #2. An indexed annuity effectively limits your choice of mutual funds to one: a stock index fund. Therefore, you cannot diversify your investment and make changes to your asset allocation like you can with a variable annuity.

Disadvantage #3. The value of your investment in an indexed annuity is subject to the financial health of the issuing insurance company. Therefore, if the insurer goes bankrupt, you could experience a loss.

Let's compare the net effect of Sheila Turner's $20,000 one-time investment in an indexed annuity to that of a variable annuity that is fully invested in an S&P 500 index fund. Assume the term of her investment is 30 years, and she is lucky enough to see the average annual price appreciation of the S&P 500 go up by a steady 7.5% with a dividend payout enhancing that return by an additional 3% per year.

	Investing in an Indexed Annuity	Investing in a Variable Annuity
Initial After-Tax Contribution	$20,000	$20,000
x Annual Total Return	x 7.5%	x (7.5 + 3.0)%
First Year Earnings	$1,500	$2,100
Investment Value after One Year	$21,500	$22,100
Investment Value after Ten Years	$41,221	$54,282
Investment Value after Thirty Years	$175,099	$399,851

As you can see, the additional 3% dividend yield available through the variable annuity S&P 500 index mutual fund provides Ms. Turner with an extra $224,752 at the end of 30 years. Moreover, if the market starts to tumble during this period, Ms. Turner has the flexibility to shift her fund allocations, thereby potentially increasing this difference even further.

Who Should Consider Indexed Annuities?

You should only consider investing through an indexed annuity if you want the potential of stock market returns but are afraid of a market decline and lack the time or ability to actively manage your investment. Bear in mind that you will not experience the full returns of other investors who are using S&P 500 index mutual funds, but you are guaranteed at least a small return on your investment regardless of what the stock market does. Just be sure you stick with an insurer that has a strong Weiss Safety Rating.

Fixed Annuities

The oldest and most conservative type of annuity is the fixed annuity. Under this type of investment, you contribute your after-tax dollars to the pooled accounts of an insurance company, and the insurer invests the money primarily in bonds, guaranteeing you a minimum annual return on your investment of 3% to 5% before deducting expenses. In their sales pitches, most insurance companies will show you illustrations assuming annual returns of 7% to 10%. But the reality is they have historically averaged a mediocre 3% to 6% after expenses.

Just as with variable annuities, fixed annuities provide the opportunity for tax-deferred investment growth, with taxes due on the earnings portion of your investment once you convert it into an immediate annuity. Unlike variable annuities, however, your investment dollars are not held in separate subaccounts, segregated from the rest of the insurance company's assets. So if you do buy a fixed annuity, keep a watchful eye on the financial health of the insurance company by periodically monitoring its Safety Rating.

Fixed immediate annuities provide you with a fixed payout which stays the same until you die or the end of the annuity's term depending on the payout option you choose. On the other hand, the payout from a variable immediate annuity will fluctuate depending on the growth you experience in your underlying mutual fund investments. This means that the purchasing power of your monthly income from a fixed annuity will decline over the years due to inflation, while the prospect of higher returns in a variable annuity has the potential to help you maintain your purchasing power if you are willing to accept the added risk.

Advantages vs. Variable Annuities

Fixed annuities are extremely low risk in that you are not directly affected by market fluctuations, as compared to variable annuities which can be risky depending on the underlying mutual funds you select. Their guaranteed minimum annual returns give you peace of mind. You know that, provided you're with a strong insurer, your deferred investment is going to grow year-in and year-out. And if you do not have an interest in actively managing your own investments, fixed annuities have a definite advantage.

Disadvantages vs. Variable Annuities

Disadvantage #l. Your annual returns are extremely limited. Historically speaking, fixed annuities have typically yielded about 2% to 6% annually compared to 11% for stock mutual funds.

Disadvantage #2. The safety of your investment is ultimately dependent on the financial health of your insurance company.

Example

The only real difference that can be illustrated by comparing a fixed annuity to a variable annuity is the difference in growth based on the expected performance of one versus the other. Aside from this, the tax implications are exactly the same for either type of investment.

Let's assume that Bill Reilly invests $20,000 under two scenarios: one using a fixed annuity returning 2.0%, and the other using a variable annuity returning 4%.

	Investing in a Fixed Annuity	Investing in a Variable Annuity
Initial After-Tax Contribution	$20,000	$20,000
x Annual Total Return	x 2%	x 4%
First Year Earnings	$400	$800
Investment Value after One Year	$20,400	$20,800
Investment Value after Ten Years	$24,380	$29,604
Investment Value after Thirty Years	$36,227	$64,868

As you can see, the 2% yield differential between the two investments would provide Mr. Reilly with an extra $28,641 at the end of 30 years. And if you rework the example based on an 11% annual return which more closely approximates the stock market's long-term historical performance, this differential widens to a whopping $421,619 at the end of 30 years. Keep in mind that the assumptions in this analysis are based on historical results which may not necessarily be indicative of future performance.

The drastic decline in the stock market during 2008 and early 2009 demonstrates the possibility of wide fluctuations in annual results. In a year such as 2008 when the S&P 500 Index was down 37%, the guaranteed rate of a fixed annuity looks pretty good. This, of course, is just one year in a long-term investment.

Who Should Consider Fixed Annuities?

Fixed annuities are most appropriate for people who have very little investment experience and do not want to assume responsibility for managing their investments. A deferred fixed annuity is a good means of steadily building a tax-deferred nest egg with very little risk (other than the risk of an insurance company failure). And an immediate fixed annuity can provide a good deal of comfort during retirement, knowing that you will receive a fixed amount every month, guaranteed for the rest of your life.

Variable Life Insurance

A variable life insurance policy is a combination of (a) regular whole life insurance, and (b) a stock market investment. These policies let you buy the life insurance you need while investing the cash value of your policy, tax-deferred, in the stock market in the hope of achieving higher growth than is normally offered through a whole life insurance policy. You get the potential for higher returns plus a fully paid policy. But you also assume a degree of market risk.

Just as with a whole life insurance policy, you make periodic fixed premium payments to cover the current cost of the insurance and to build up your cash value. Once your cash value is sufficient to cover the insurance costs for the remainder of your actuarial expected life span, you stop making premium payments and the annual insurance costs get deducted from your cash value. Also, you can borrow against the cash value of a variable life policy at the interest rate stated in your policy contract.

Like a variable annuity, variable life gives you the ability to invest the cash value of your policy in the various mutual fund subaccounts offered by the insurance company. Assuming you are able to invest wisely, this will allow you to grow your cash value more quickly so that your insurance policy can be paid up sooner. You can usually switch your investment between funds with a phone call (typically limited to 12 free trades per year); and because you are using subaccounts, the cash value of your policy is not at risk in the event of a failure. The life insurance portion, however, is at risk in a failure.

But remember: A variable life policy is a life insurance policy - not a retirement savings vehicle like annuities. Therefore, the overall costs are going to be higher in order to pay for the insurance coverage you have purchased.

Advantages vs. Variable Annuities

Advantage #1. You get a life insurance policy. If this is what you want, it's an advantage.

Advantage #2. You can borrow against the cash value in your policy, which can come in handy in times of emergency.

Disadvantages vs. Variable Annuities

Disadvantage #1. Since you are paying for a life insurance policy, your costs will be higher; and your net returns, lower. If you don't need life insurance, this is a disadvantage.

Disadvantage #2. You have to stick to a fixed premium contribution schedule; whereas with a variable annuity, you can invest as much as you like, whenever you like.

Who Should Consider Variable Life Insurance?

If you (a) need life insurance and (b) are willing to accept the added responsibility and risk of stock market investing, a variable life insurance policy might be right for you. However, if you already have a variable life policy and you are no longer in need of insurance, you may want to consider converting the cash value of your policy into a variable annuity. Contact your insurance agent and inquire about a tax-free 1035 exchange. He or she will be able to help you from there.

Variable Universal Life Insurance

This is basically the same as variable life insurance with one key difference: A variable universal life policy allows you to vary the amount of your annual premium contribution or suspend it altogether, if you choose. As a result, the cash value and amount of insurance coverage will fluctuate, depending on the adequacy of your premium payments.

Other than that, a variable universal life policy and variable life policy are essentially the same. Both allow you to invest the cash value of your policy in a selection of mutual fund subaccounts, where it will grow tax-free. And both allow you to borrow against the accumulated cash value in your policy. Thus a variable universal life policy has the same advantages and disadvantages versus a variable annuity as a variable life policy would.

Who Should Consider Variable Universal Life?

If you (a) need life insurance, (b) are willing to accept the risk of the stock market investing, but (c) are unwilling to commit to a fixed annual premium payment, you should consider a variable universal life policy. As with a variable life policy, if you already have a variable universal life policy and you no longer need the insurance, consider converting the cash value of your policy into a variable annuity.

Summary

Don't consider purchasing a variable annuity until you first take advantage of company-sponsored retirement plans and IRAs. Then, if you need additional investments in order to save enough money for retirement, take a look at the tax-deferred choices available to you.

Depending on your level of stock market expertise and risk tolerance, you may find variable annuities to be just the thing. And if the concept of variable annuity investing sounds attractive but you lack the time or inclination to get personally involved, you may want to consider hiring a financial planner or money manager to handle things for you.

If variable annuities sound too risky, a fixed annuity or indexed annuity will probably suit you better. Just don't forget to periodically monitor the financial safety of the issuing insurance company. Otherwise, you're taking unnecessary chances with your retirement nest egg.

Whatever you do, *always shop around* and compare one investment to another. There's absolutely no reason to incur high costs or suffer with poor returns when there are plenty of good alternatives out there.

Glossary

401(k) Plan	A company-sponsored retirement savings plan that allows participants to make pre-tax contributions up to 100% of their annual salary or a maximum of $18,500 in 2018 ($24,500 if age 50 or older). These contributions grow tax-deferred until they are paid out, at which time the participant owes taxes on the amounts received.
After-Tax Contribution	A contribution made to fund an investment which has no tax benefit in the year in which the contribution is made.
Annuitize	To convert a deferred annuity into an immediate annuity and select a payout option whereby you will receive periodic payments. See also "Deferred Annuity" and "Immediate Annuity."
Annuity	An investment in the form of an insurance company policy where after-tax dollars are contributed, but any subsequent earnings are tax-deferred. See also "Deferred Annuity" and "Immediate Annuity."
Deferred Annuity	Any annuity that is in the build-up stage where you are making contributions but are not receiving regular payments. This applies to any type of annuity including a fixed annuity, variable annuity, or indexed annuity. See also "Immediate Annuity."
Fixed Annuity	An annuity whose rate of return is based on the performance achieved by the issuing company's bond investments. This type of annuity also offers a minimum guaranteed annual growth rate.
Front-End Load	A charge paid by the investor that is deducted from his or her investment value at the time the investment is funded. This charge is typically assessed to cover commissions paid to the person selling the investment. Not all investments levy a front-end load.
Indexed Annuity	An annuity whose rate of return is based on the price appreciation of the S&P 500 stock index, without dividends. This type of annuity also offers a minimum guaranteed annual growth rate. Also called Equity-Indexed Annuity.
Immediate Annuity	Any annuity that is in the payout stage where you are receiving periodic payments over the course of the remainder of your life or some predefined period.

Insurance Cost	That portion of an annuity or life insurance policy's costs that cover the actuarial risk of the policy to the insurance company.
IRA	Individual Retirement Account. A retirement savings vehicle usually funded with pre-tax contributions that allows an investment to grow tax deferred. See also "Roth IRA."
Marginal Tax Rate	The rate at which a person is taxed on each incremental dollar of income. In other words, the amount of income taxes owed on the last dollar earned.
Mutual Fund	An investment owned by a group of investors who have pooled their monies. A mutual fund's prospectus defines the investment strategy it is obligated to follow, along with any other special provisions for loads, expenses or other fees.
Mutual Fund Annual Expenses	The expenses paid by a mutual fund to cover the mutual fund manager's compensation and other administrative costs.
Mutual Fund Subaccount	Mutual funds that are kept in the policy owner's name instead of being pooled (see also "Pooled Accounts"). These investments are not considered part of the assets of the managing company so that if the company were to fail, the mutual fund subaccounts would not be at risk of loss. However, they would be frozen for a period of time until the bankruptcy judge assigned another company to take over the obligations of the failed company. Variable annuities, variable life, and variable universal life policies are all examples of policies offering mutual fund subaccounts.
No-Load, No Surrender Charge	A feature noted by investments that do not charge you a fee upon initiating or withdrawing the investment.
Pooled Accounts	The situation wherein an insurance company takes the premiums paid in by a group of policy owners onto its books and creates a large pool of assets which it then invests and manages. The pooled assets are considered assets of the insurance company such that if the insurer were to fail, the policy owners would be at risk of loss of the value in their investments. Insurance policies using pooled accounts include whole life policies, universal life policies, fixed annuities, and indexed annuities.
Pre-Tax Contributions	Contributions made to fund an investment where the amount of the contribution is not counted as income in the current tax year.

Principal	The actual amount contributed into an investment, not including any monies earned from the investment itself.
Roth IRA	Introduced in tax year 1998 and modified in 2001, this type of IRA is funded with after-tax contributions, allowing the investor to withdraw tax-free principal and earnings at a later date.
S&P 500 Index	A barometer of the stock market based on the 500 largest publicly traded firms in terms of market capitalization. Since it is impractical for an individual investor to own such a large and diverse group of equities, some mutual funds attempt to mimic the stocks included in this index to achieve comparable performance.
Subaccount	See "Mutual Fund Subaccount."
Surrender Charge	A charge or load paid by the investor that is deducted from his or her investment value at the time the investment is withdrawn. This charge is typically used as a deterrent to making early withdrawals and is thus usually phased out within the first few years after the investment has been funded. Not all investments levy a surrender charge.
Tax-Deferred	The situation wherein the income and/or capital gains from an investment are not subject to income taxes in the year earned, but may be subject to income taxes at a later date.
Tax-Free	The situation wherein no taxes are owed on the investment or its earnings.
Variable Annuity	An annuity that permits the policy owner to invest in a selection of mutual funds through separate mutual fund subaccounts.
Variable Life	A life insurance policy where the policy owner pays fixed premium amounts to the insurance company and is permitted to invest the cash value of the policy in a selection of mutual funds through separate mutual fund subaccounts.
Variable Universal Life	A life insurance policy where the policy owner can vary the premium amounts paid to the insurance company and is permitted to invest the cash value of the policy in a selection of mutual funds through separate mutual fund subaccounts.
Whole Life	A life insurance policy where the policy owner pays fixed premium amounts into a pooled account managed by the insurance company.